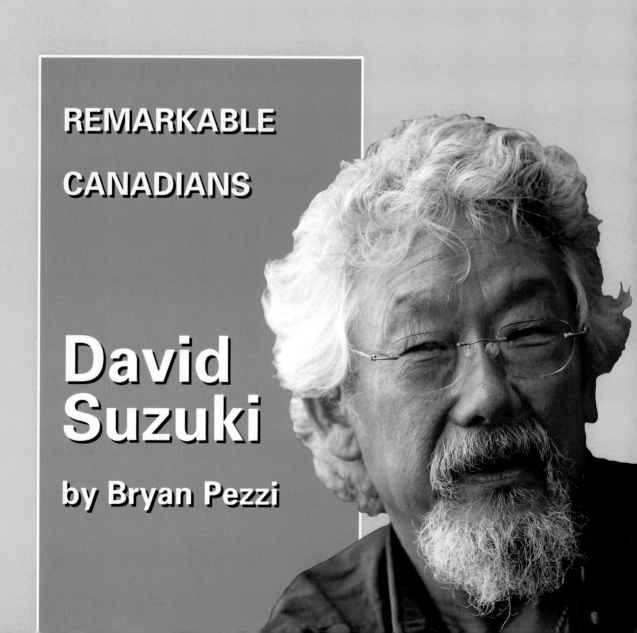

REMARKABLE

CANADIANS

David Suzuki

by Bryan Pezzi

Published by Weigl Educational Publishers Limited
6325 – 10 Street SE
Calgary, Alberta, Canada
T2H 2Z9

Web site: www.weigl.ca

Library and Archives Canada Cataloguing in Publication

Pezzi, Bryan
      David Suzuki / Bryan Pezzi.

(Remarkable Canadians)
Includes index.
ISBN 1-55388-209-1 (bound).--ISBN 1-55388-213-X (pbk.)
      1. Suzuki, David, 1936- --Juvenile literature. 2. Environmentalists--Canada--Biography--
Juvenile literature. 3. Geneticists-- Canada--Biography. 4. Authors, Canadian (English)--20th
century--Biography--Juvenile literature. 5. Broadcasts--Canada--Biography--Juvenile
literature. I. Title. II. Series: Canadian biographies (Calgary, Alta.)

GE56.S99P49 2006   j333.72'092   C2006-900921-X

Printed in the United States of America
1 2 3 4 5 6 7 8 9 0 10 09 08 07 06

Editor: Frances Purslow
Design: Terry Paulhus

We acknowledge the financial support of the Government of Canada through the Book
Publishing Industry Development Program (BPIDP) for our publishing activities.

Cover: David Suzuki has written dozens of books and hosted several television shows. He
continues to try to help the environment.

Photograph Credits
Cover: CP (Larry MacDougal); British Columbia Archives: page 16 (B-06069); CP (Larry
MacDougal): page 1; CP (Tim Krochak): page 5; Photographs from *David Suzuki: The
Autobiography*, by David Suzuki, published 2006 by Greystone Books, a division of Douglas &
McIntyre Ltd. Reprinted by permission of the author and the publisher: pages 6, 8, 14;
Courtesy of David Suzuki: pages 9, 10, 19, 20; Copyright © Province of British of Columbia.
All rights reserved. Reprinted with permission of the Province of British Columbia.
www.ipp.gov.bc.ca: page 7 top left.

Every reasonable effort has been made to trace ownership and to obtain permission to reprint
copyright material. The publishers would be pleased to have any errors or omissions brought
to their attention so that they may be corrected in subsequent printings.

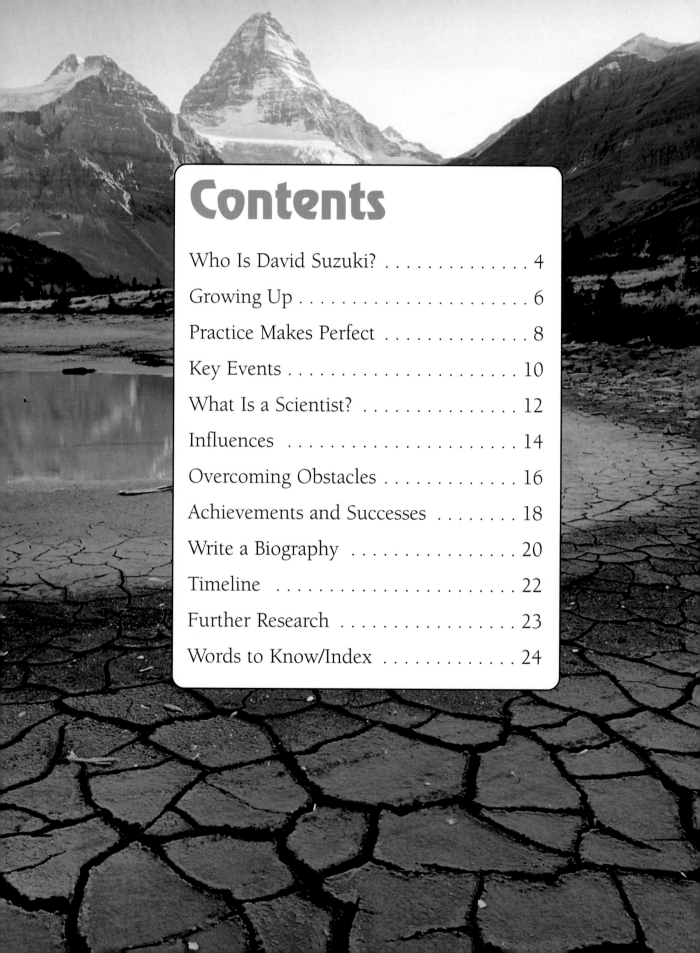

Contents

Who Is David Suzuki?

Dr. David Suzuki is a scientist. Many scientists are not very well known. David is different because he appears on television. His most successful television show is *The Nature of Things*. On the show, David explains science in a way that is fun and easy to learn. David helps people learn about the environment, too. In 1990, he started the David Suzuki Foundation. This group works to protect nature. Today, David works to help the environment. He also writes newspaper stories and books and hosts radio shows.

"The battle to save Mother Earth remains urgent and must continue."

David Suzuki

Growing Up

On March 24, 1936, David Takayoshi Suzuki was born in Vancouver, British Columbia. David's parents ran a dry-cleaning shop in the Marpole neighbourhood. The family lived in an apartment in the back of the shop. David was the only boy in the family. He had a twin sister and two younger sisters. As a young boy, David enjoyed nature.

David's family was Japanese Canadian. His grandparents were from Japan, and his parents were both born in Canada. Although the Suzukis were Canadian, they faced **discrimination**. Japanese Canadians could not vote or hold certain jobs. In 1939, when David was 3 years old, World War II began. It continued until 1945. During the war, Canada and Japan were on opposite sides. As a result, Japanese Canadians, such as the Suzuki family, were sent to **internment camps**. David's family lived in a camp from 1942 until the end of the war.

🍁 David and his twin sister, Marcia, attended their first day of kindergarten in Vancouver, in September 1941.

British Columbia Tidbits

COAT OF ARMS

TREE
Western Red Cedar

FLOWER
Pacific Dogwood

Victoria is the provincial capital.

British Columbia is bordered by the Pacific Ocean on the west coast.

British Columbia was the sixth province to join **Confederation**.

Vancouver is the largest city in the province.

There are more than 4 million people living in British Columbia.

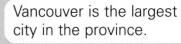

Think about it!

British Columbia is the province where David Suzuki was born. It is also the province where he lives today. Research the province's environment. How might the environment have influenced David's career?

Practice Makes Perfect

David loved nature from an early age. He liked to spend time outdoors with his father. Together, they fished and explored forests and lakes. David's father would point out animals, birds, trees, and other plants. When David was older, his family moved to London, Ontario. There, David explored the nature of Point Pelee and the swamps around the city. Sometimes he collected insects and made displays of them.

🍁 David enjoyed fishing with his father in the lakes near Slocan, British Columbia.

David's parents wanted him to be a good student. They helped him learn to speak in public. He entered his first speech contest when he was Grade 10. He won first prize. David won many more speech contests after that. Public speaking helped David win a place on his school's student council. In his senior year of high school, David ran for school president. This was hard work because most of the students did not know much about him. David won the election because he spoke well and had good ideas.

QUICK FACTS

- David became a professor of **zoology** at age 33.

- In 1972, David was named outstanding Japanese Canadian of the year.

- *The Nature of Things* has aired on Canadian Broadcasting Corporation (CBC) television for more than 30 years.

David did not want to run for school president because he thought he would lose. His dad convinced him to try. He told David, "Whatever you do, there will always be people better than you, but that doesn't mean you shouldn't try."

Key Events

After David became a scientist, he made important scientific discoveries. He became well known in the world of science.

In 1962, David made his first appearance on television. CBC TV asked him to host some shows about science. Soon, he had his own television program. It was called *Suzuki on Science*. After that, he hosted *Science Magazine* and a radio show called *Quirks and Quarks*. In 1979, David began work on *The Nature of Things*. This television show made David a star. The program aired in 83 countries. In 1985, David worked on another show. It was called *A Planet for the Taking*. About 1.8 million viewers tuned in every week.

David sometimes writes for newspapers. He is also the author of more than 35 science books. In 2006, David wrote a book about his own life. It is called *David Suzuki: the Autobiography*.

David has written children's books about the environment, such as *You Are the Earth* and *If We Could See the Air*.

Thoughts from David

David's love of nature led him to a career in science. Here are some things he has said about his life.

Japan attacks Pearl Harbor, December 7, 1941.

"...Pearl Harbor was the single most important event shaping my life..."

David studies science in university.

"[Science] involves going where your curiosity leads you..."

Growing up, David forms a close bond with his father.

"My father was my inspiration, my hero, my model."

David studies the **genetics** of fruit flies.

"I was a full-fledged scientist and wasn't afraid to work hard and long."

David visits Japan in 1968.

"For the first time in my life, I was surrounded by people who all looked like me."

David attends high school in London, Ontario.

"At school, I had a few friends, but none of us was part of the in-crowd."

David appears on his own television show.

"I can't see the people I'm trying to reach, but I know they're there. I meet them all across Canada."

What is a Scientist?

David is a scientist. A scientist is a person who studies the natural world. David is a special kind of scientist called a geneticist. People in this field study genes. A gene is part of a special code found inside the **cells** of every living thing. This code gives animals and plants their special **traits**.

Scientists perform experiments to prove their ideas. Scientists spend much of their time doing research. They ask questions about nature and then try to find answers. In Canada, a scientist might work in a university, or a hospital, or for a business. Some scientists try to cure illness. Others make inventions to improve people's lives. There are many branches of science and different kinds of scientists.

❉ Scientists often work in laboratories where they perform experiments.

Scientist 101

Sir Frederic Banting (1891–1941)

Field of Study Medicine (the study of the human body and disease)

Achievements Frederic worked with his partner, Charles Best. They discovered a **hormone** called insulin. People with a disease called diabetes use insulin to stay healthy. Thanks to Frederic's discovery, these people can lead healthier lives.

Awards Nobel Prize, 1923.

Biruté Galdikas (1946–)

Field of Study Anthropology (the study of how humans have developed)

Achievements Biruté studies orangutans. These are large apes that live in the jungle. Biruté goes to the rain forest to study these animals in their natural **habitat**.

Awards PETA Humanitarian Award, 1990; Eddie Bauer Hero of the Earth Award, 1991; Sierra Club Chico Mendes Award, 1992; United Nations Global 500 Award 1993; Tyler Prize (University of Southern California), 1997.

Roberta Bondar (1945–)

Field of Study Neurology (the study of the brain)

Achievements Roberta is a scientist who specializes in neurology. She studies how the brain works with the eyes to let people see. Roberta is also Canada's first female astronaut. In 1992, she flew on the space shuttle *Discovery*. She studied how the human body works in space.

Awards NASA Space Medal; Member of the Canadian Medical Hall of Fame; Officer of the Order of Canada; Fellow of the Royal Society of Canada; named to the International Women's Forum Hall of Fame.

David Levy (1948–)

Field of Study Astronomy (the study of stars and planets)

Achievements David studies comets. These are balls of ice and dust that move through space. In 1993, along with Gene and Carolyn Shoemaker, David discovered a comet. The comet was named Shoemaker-Levy 9 in their honour. This comet became famous in July 1994, when it crashed into the planet Jupiter. This was an important event. No one had ever seen a comet crash into a planet before.

Awards Several comets have been named after David.

The Microscope

Scientists use many tools to help them study nature. One of these tools is the microscope. This device uses a lens to allow people to see very small things. Some things are too small to see with the naked eye. These include cells, **bacteria**, and some very tiny plants and animals.

Influences

The greatest influence in David's life was his father. Although David's father was named Kaoru Suzuki, everyone called him Carr. Carr's parents moved from Japan to Canada before he was born. As a child, Carr learned the Japanese customs of his family. He also had to learn the Canadian way of life.

When he reached adulthood, Carr married Setsu and had four children. David was the only son. He had a special bond with his father.

David's parents, Setsu and Carr Kaoru Suzuki, were married for 50 years.

David thought his dad was a hero. He gained a love of nature from his father. Carr taught David all about plants and animals. They would spend time outdoors together.

Carr also taught David the importance of education and hard work. These were important lessons. They helped David succeed as a student and as a scientist.

🍁 The USS *California* was one of the U.S. battleships bombed by Japanese attack planes in Pearl Harbor during World War II.

PEARL HARBOR

Pearl Harbor is on Oahu Island, in Hawai'i. It used to be a base for U.S. battleships. On December 7, 1941, Japanese airplanes attacked Pearl Harbor. Ships were destroyed, and many people died. After this event, the United States went to war with Japan. Life became difficult for Japanese people living in North America.

Overcoming Obstacles

David Suzuki has faced some hardships in the early part of his life. However, they did not stop him from achieving success. As a Japanese Canadian, David has experienced **racism**. When David was only 6 years old, he and his family were forced to move. This happened because Canada was at war with Japan. All Japanese Canadians were moved away from the coast of British Columbia, and many of their belongings were taken from them.

David's family were sent to a camp in the Slocan Valley. Their new home was crowded and dirty. Most of the children spoke Japanese, but David only spoke English. It was difficult for David to make friends. Schooling was a problem, too. There was no school during David's first year in the camp.

Many Japanese Canadians were forced to move into abandoned towns in the Slocan Valley during World War II.

David began Grade 1 when he was 7 years old. Although he began late, he did well in his studies. He completed Grades 1, 2, and 3 in just 1 year. After 3 years, David's family left the camp. They moved to Ontario, where David attended a regular school. He was a good student there also. After high school, David went to university. He received degrees in **biology** and zoology.

After graduating high school, David earned a scholarship to study biology at Amherst College in Massachusetts.

Achievements and Successes

David has succeeded in many areas of his life. He has made great achievements in science, **broadcasting**, and **activism**. David's work has won many awards and honours.

David earned science degrees in Massachusetts and Illinois. Then, his work took him to Tennessee, Alberta, and British Columbia. At the University of British Columbia, David ran the biggest genetics lab in Canada. He became known for his research. From 1969 to 1971, David won annual awards for the best Canadian scientist under the age of 35.

🍁 *The Nature of Things with David Suzuki* has won many awards, including Best Educational Value Award at the International Wildlife Film Festival and the Science and Society Journalism Award for Best Television Item.

In the 1970s, David became a **celebrity**. Millions of viewers watched his television programs. He used his fame to teach people about important issues regarding the environment. In 1976, he won the **Order of Canada**. Ten years later, the **United Nations** gave David an award for helping people to understand science. David also works to solve environmental issues that affect Aboriginal Peoples.

THE DAVID SUZUKI FOUNDATION

In 1990, David and his wife started the David Suzuki Foundation. The group is based in Vancouver, British Columbia. There are about 40,000 members. The foundation works to protect nature. It does research on problems facing Earth. The foundation sends out newsletters, brochures, and information kits about these problems.

To find out more, visit:
www.davidsuzuki.org

Today, David lives in Vancouver with his wife, Dr. Tara Cullis. David still tries to help the environment. He has started his own environmental organization. He also writes a weekly newspaper column. David gives speeches all over the world. Some people do not agree with David's strong views. He stands up for his beliefs, even when others are against him. In 2005, David won a Canadian Environment Award for his lifetime of work.

❧ David loves to spend time with his two youngest daughters, Severn and Sarika.

Write a Biography

Some people have very interesting lives. They may overcome problems or achieve great success. A person's life story can be the subject of a book. This kind of a book is called a biography. There are many biographies in a library. The biographies describe the lives of movie stars, athletes, and great leaders. These people may be alive today, or they may have lived many years ago. Reading a biography can help you learn more about a person.

At school, you might be asked to write a biography review. First, decide who you want to write about. You can choose a scientist, such as David Suzuki, or any other person you find interesting. Then, find out if your library has any books about this person. Learn as much as you can about him or her. Write down the key events in this person's life. What was this person's childhood like? What has he or she accomplished? What are his or her goals? What makes this person special or unusual?

A concept web is a useful research tool. Read the questions in the following concept web. Answer the questions in your notebook. Your answers will help you write your biography review.

- What did you learn from the book?
- Would you suggest this book to others?
- Was anything missing from the book?

- Where does this individual currently reside?
- Does he or she have a family?

- Where and when was this person born?
- Describe his or her parents, siblings, and friends.
- Did this person grow up in unusual circumstances?

Your Opinion

Adulthood

Childhood

REVIEWING A BIOGRAPHY

Main Accomplishments

Help and Obstacles

Work and Preparation

- What is this person's life's work?
- Has he or she received awards or recognition for accomplishments?
- How have this person's accomplishments served others?

- What was this person's education?
- What was his or her work experience?
- How does this person work; what is or was the process he or she uses or used?

- Did this individual have a positive attitude?
- Did he or she receive assistance from others?
- Did this person have a **mentor**?
- Did this person face any hardships?
- If so, how were the hardships overcome?

Timeline

DECADE	DAVID SUZUKI	WORLD EVENTS
1930s	David is born on March 24, 1936, in Vancouver.	The period from 1929 to the early 1940s was known as the Great Depression. There were few goods to buy and many people lost their jobs, homes, and money.
1940s	David and his family live in the internment camps from 1942 to 1945.	On December 7, 1941, Japanese planes attack Pearl Harbor.
1950s	In 1958, David graduates from Amherst College with an honours degree in biology.	On June 2, 1953, Elizabeth II becomes queen of the British Commonwealth.
1960s	David does genetic research with fruit flies.	First Nations people of Canada win the right to vote in federal elections.
1970s	In 1979, David begins hosting *The Nature of Things*.	The 1976 summer Olympics are held in Montreal, Quebec.
1990s	In 1990, David and his wife, Dr. Tara Cullis, start the David Suzuki Foundation.	In 1996, Dolly the sheep becomes the first animal to be **cloned** successfully.
2000s	In 2004, David is chosen by CBC viewers as one of the 10 greatest Canadians.	In 2005, Canada starts following the Kyoto Protocol, a plan to reduce **pollution**.

Further Research

How can I find out more about David Suzuki?

Most libraries have computers that connect to a database for searching for information. If you input a key word, you will be provided with a list of books in the library that contain information on that topic. Non-fiction books are arranged numerically, using their call number. Fiction books are organized alphabetically by the author's last name.

Websites

To learn more about the David Suzuki Foundation, visit www.davidsuzuki.org

To learn more about Canadian science and scientists, visit www.science.ca

Television

The Nature of Things with David Suzuki airs on CBC television. (Check your local listings.)

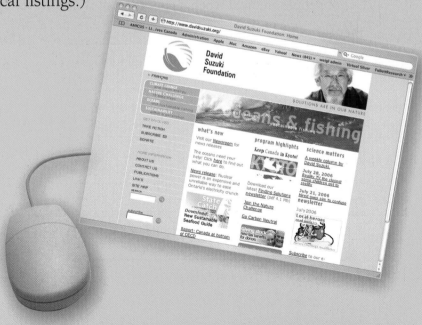

Words to Know

activism: working for a cause or an issue

bacteria: simple life forms that are too small to see without a microscope

biology: the study of living things

broadcasting: making programs on television or radio

celebrity: someone who is famous

cells: the smallest parts of any living thing

cloned: made an exact copy of a living being

Confederation: the creation of Canada in 1867

discrimination: treating people differently because of their race

genetics: the study of genes, the code inside cells that gives living things their special traits

habitat: the kind of environment where an animal or plant makes its homes

hormone: a chemical that is produced inside the body

internment camps: places where certain groups of people are held when a country is at war

mentor: a wise and trusted teacher

Order of Canada: a special award for Canadians who have made a major difference to Canada

pollution: anything that makes the environment dirty or unhealthy

racism: treating people poorly because they are a different race

traits: qualities

United Nations: an organization made up of most of the countries in the world

zoology: the study of animals

Index